中国科幻小说精选·中英对照

新诺亚方舟
THE NEW NOAH'S ARK

刘兴诗　著
温绍贤　译
［英］蒂娜·巴莱　审校

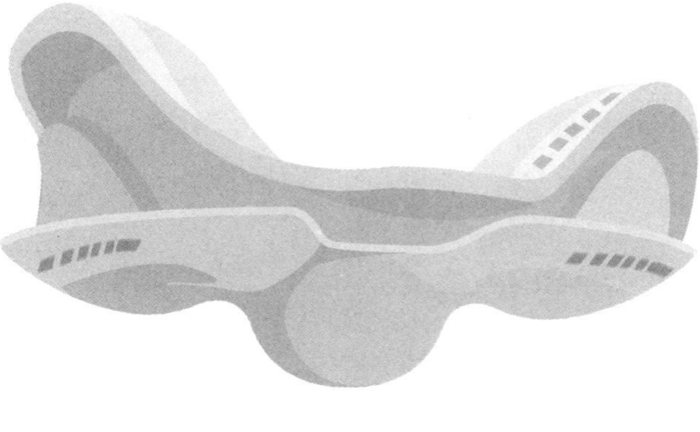

科学普及出版社
·北京·

图书在版编目（CIP）数据

新诺亚方舟：中英对照/刘兴诗著；温绍贤译．—北京：科学普及出版社，2014.6
（中国科幻小说精选）
ISBN 978-7-110-08625-4

Ⅰ．①新… Ⅱ．①刘… ②温… Ⅲ．①英语—汉语—对照读物 ②儿童文学—科学幻想小说—作品集—中国—当代 Ⅳ．①H319.4：Ⅰ

中国版本图书馆CIP数据核字(2014)第099048号

出版人	苏　青
责任编辑	单　亭　张　莉
封面设计	银搏时代
责任校对	王勤杰
责任印制	张建农

出　　版	科学普及出版社
发　　行	科学普及出版社发行部
地　　址	北京市海淀区中关村南大街16号
邮　　编	100081
发行电话	010-62173865
传　　真	010-62179148
网　　址	http://www.cspbooks.com.cn

开　　本	880mm×1230mm　1/32
字　　数	41千字
印　　张	2.5
印　　数	1—5000册
版　　次	2014年8月第1版
印　　次	2014年8月第1次印刷
印　　刷	北京盛通印刷股份有限公司
书　　号	ISBN 978-7-110-08625-4 / H·210
定　　价	16.00元

CONTENTS

目录

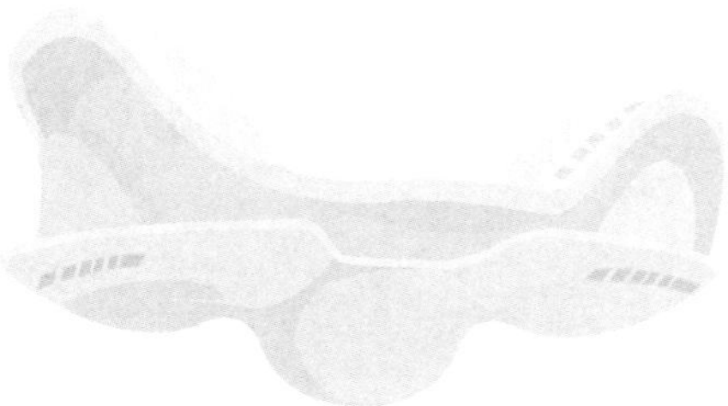

前言：太空浪游记第一篇

我，阿里·赛义德·辛伯达，从巴索拉机场扬起飞船的太阳帆，飞上宇宙太空啦！临行的时候，年迈的妈妈泪眼婆娑地望着我。许多亲密的朋友都紧紧地握住我的手，对我说："辛伯达，快打消你的脑瓜子里的这个古怪念头吧！太空里没有可口的羊肉馅饼，也没有阴凉的椰枣树。那儿一片黑暗，充满了寂寞、寒冷和致命的危险，甚至安拉的使者也从来不光顾那些遥远的阴暗角落。弄不好你会像你那著名的同名祖先（指《一千零一夜》中的水手辛伯达，他曾经从波斯湾内的巴索拉港出发，历尽艰险，在海上做了七次航行）一样，遭遇种种不测的灾难。与其这样担惊受怕，倒不如安安稳稳地坐在巴格达的家里，享受人世间的天伦乐趣。"

可是，当年我正年少气盛，胸膛里跳跃着一颗愚蠢透顶的好奇心，血管里燃烧着渴求探索和发现的炽热的火焰，对我们这个狭窄的星球上的生活早就感到厌倦了。试问，

FOREWORD: THE FIRST STORY OF ADVENTURES IN THE OUTER SPACE

I, Ali-Sa'id Sindbad by name, hoisted the sun-sails of my spaceship in readiness for taking off into the space at Basalla Airport. Before I started, my old mother said nothing, but just gazed at me with tears in her eyes. Many good friends shook me by the hand, and said: "Sindbad, do give up this ridiculous idea. You won't find anything pleasant in the space — no mutton pies, no shady date palms to lie under! Space is dark, solitary, cold, and deadly dangerous. Even Allah's envoy never visited those remote and dark corners. If you don't do a good job there, you will probably suffer all manner of unforeseen disasters, just like your unfortunate well-known ancestor whose name you bear. He set out from Basalla Port in Persian Gulf and made seven voyages in the sea and suffered a lot during his voyages. Much better for you to stay at home in Baghdad and lead a normal happy life with your own family."

At the time I was young and full of energy, and my foolish head was bursting with curiosity: I yearned to be an explorer and make exciting discoveries. The life in our earth which offered me limited scope bored me long ago. Should I

除了神秘的太空外，我还能到哪儿去溜达？难道还要去沉闷的红海、枯燥乏味的北极冰场或印度洋底的水下迷宫，寻求生活的乐趣和刺激吗？

不，古老的地球已经像沙漠里的金字塔似的丧失了一切神秘感。对一个充满热烈的理想和勇气的新一代的青年来说，只有广袤无边的宇宙才是唯一的出路。说真的，那时我整天都沉溺在五彩缤纷的幻梦里，一心指望能一下子就发现一大串没有人知道的新星球，用亲爱的故乡巴格达，以及妈妈和我的名字给它一一命名。唉，我那死心眼儿的老妈妈呀！您可懂得孩子真诚挚爱您的心？我将要通过自己的冒险活动，来为您在天空中取得一个永恒的星座位置，那该有多好！

噢，我实在是太激动了，兴冲冲地拉开了启动阀，只来得及回头挥了挥手，就一溜烟飞进了无边无际的宇宙太空。想不到为了满足幼稚的好奇心，我终于为此吃尽了种种难以形容的苦头。

如今当我重新握笔安坐在巴格达的家中，一面喝着妈

look for life, pleasure, and excitement in the Red Sea, or the monotonous ice fields of the North Pole, or the undersea labyrinth of the Indian Ocean?

No! The old earth is like the pyramids in the desert, and it had lost all its mystery. To a go-ahead young man like me, courageous and imaginative, the only choice was the vastness of space: it was that or nothing. I indulged in the rosiest dreams, seeing myself as the discoverer of a whole string of new planets previously unknown to mankind. I would name them after my dear native town of Baghdad, after my mother, and after myself. Oh, my stubborn old mother! You should have known how much of my ambition sprang from love of you – how I longed to win eternal fame amongst the stars for you by my adventures.

I was far too excited. I started the engine. I just had time to turn my head and shout goodbye to them all as my spaceship rose into air and then to the boundless space. I never really believed that my childish curiosity would result in my enduring serious suffering.

Now, as I sit safely at home in Baghdad writing this, drinking

妈端送在面前的热气腾腾的鲜羊奶，一面抬头眺望耸立在窗外街心广场上的水手辛伯达的花岗石像时，不禁思绪起伏，感慨万端。是的，我也曾和他一样，不多不少地离乡背井做了七次冒险航行，见识过不少异星球的风土人情。可是远航给我带来了什么好处呢？只是如今我才深深明白，除了我们脚下的古老大地外，宇宙空间里并没有任何理想中的乐园。如果说我在这些航行中也曾有所收获的话，那就是一连串使人永远难以忘怀的教训。啊，万能的真主，请您大发慈悲，千万别让我们的星球也蒙受那些遥远的天外世界所遭受的不幸吧！

亲爱的朋友们，从这一点出发，我奉献给你们的，就不仅是一些离奇古怪的故事了。记得阿拉伯国家的一位先哲曾经说过："在怪诞的神话里，也许寓有一颗严肃的心。"当你们仔细读完这一篇篇回忆录的时候，就会领悟到这的确是一句颠扑不破的至理名言！

现在，请您赏光先倾听我的第一次宇宙航行的故事吧！

a mug of steaming hot fresh goat's milk brought me by my mother, and looking through the window at the marble statue of Sindbad the Sailor in the Central Square, all sorts of feelings well up in my mind. Like him, I have left home seven times to make voyages of adventure, and it is true that I have learned a lot of the local conditions and customs of some other planets. But what benefits have my space flights brought me? Only the full realization that this old earth under my feet is the best place to be – there are no ideal paradises in space. If I have gained anything from those adventures of my youth, it is a series of unforgettable lessons. Oh omnipotent Allah, I beg you to have pity on us and save our world from suffering the same miserable fates as those planets in outer space.

Dear readers, taking this as the starting point, you should bear in mind that what I am going to tell you is not just a series of marvellous tales. I remember an Arabian sage once said, "There may be a serious heart in the most fantastic fairy tales". When you have finished reading these memoirs of mine, you will appreciate the irrefutable truth of those golden words.

This, then, is the story of my first space flight.

可恶的长尾人

我无法用恰当的语言来形容刚飞进太空时的兴奋心情。蔚蓝的阿拉伯晴空，在我的眼前一下子就幻化成无边无际的宇宙长夜。这儿那儿，到处缀饰着成列成串的璀璨明星。由于没有空气这个顽皮精灵的捉弄，它们变得更加星光灿烂，再也不无缘无故地眨巴着眼睛，仿佛都换了一张张陌生面孔似的，予人以一种特殊的新鲜感觉。我怀着无限欢愉的心情熄灭了发动机，把安装在飞船顶上的一面金属薄膜大帆升得更高，任随万能的太阳用它那无所不在的光压推动着飞船，朝向迷迷茫茫的晨空深处飘去。

我记不清飞行了多少日子，说不完曾从飞船的舷窗里朝外眺见了多少幅太空奇景。终于有一天，一颗陌生的星星出现在我的飞行轨道上，在我的面前越变越大。我选择了一块平地降落下去。

它给我的第一印象是满意的。这儿有连绵起伏的山冈，闪烁着翡翠般碧绿亮光的湖泊和河流，比我的阿拉伯

THE DETESTABLE LONG-TAILED CREATURES

My feelings as I first headed into space were beyond all description. As I watched, the bright blue sky over Arabia was gradually revealed as a boundless cosmic night studded with brilliant stars. Away from the mischievous interference of the earth's atmosphere, they no longer winked and twinkled, but shone with a steady brilliance. They looked entirely different, and they rendered me a wonderful and refreshed feeling just to gaze at them. With boundless joy I cut the engine and lifted higher the huge sail made of metal film spread above my spaceship, letting the omnipresent light pressure of the omnipotent sun propel it onwards deep into the vast and hazy realms of space.

I cannot remember now how many days I flew on, and how many strange scenes passed by outside my porthole. Then one day an uncharted planet appeared on my flight path, growing larger and larger as I headed towards it. I chose a flat piece of ground, and landed on it.

My first impression was very favourable. There were rolling hills, and lakes and rivers glistening dark green like jade.

故乡更加惹人喜爱。

“这是宇宙海洋中的一座青葱的小岛。在我的航程中首先遇见它，准是一个好兆头！”我乐滋滋地想道。

可是，噢——，当我打开飞船的舱门，刚踏下一只脚时，这个甜蜜蜜的印象立刻颠倒过来了，一大群尖嘴蚊子密密匝匝地猛扑上来，立刻在我的面孔和手臂上叮了许多青皮疙瘩，加上四周一阵阵吵闹个不停的昆虫鸣叫声，弄得人心烦意乱，欣赏风景的兴致一下子就烟消云散了。至于风景嘛，我这才看清楚。几乎所有的树木都被虫蛀坏了，枝头的树叶稀稀拉拉，黄不黄、绿不绿的，非常难看。不知这里有没有专门除虫的啄木鸟，它们都躲到哪儿去了？

“这准是安拉的疏忽，”我想，“为什么要在这个美丽的星球上，撒下这么多讨厌的小虫子？”

我捂着脑袋往前走了一段路，越来越感到有些不对劲儿。为什么在碧净如洗的天空中，竟没有一只雀鸟？唉，现在要是有一只燕子，哪怕是小麻雀也好，准能把眼前这群死死纠缠我的毒蚊消灭得一干二净。

It was more attractive than my native Arabia.

"A small green island in the ocean of space! It must be a good omen that I have first found it on my space voyage." I thought happily.

I opened the module door and climbed out. However, no sooner had one of my feet touched the ground than my good impression was hastily modified. A thick swarm of mosquito-like insects attacked me from all directions, and my face and arms instantly began to swell from their bites. I was further annoyed by a ceaseless hum of innumerable other sorts of insects all around me. My enjoyment of the beautiful scenery quickly evaporated; and indeed, now that I looked more closely at the scenery I could see that almost all the trees were damaged, evidently moth-eaten – their leaves sparse and withered. I wondered whether there were any birds like woodpeckers here, expert at catching insects, and if so where they had hidden themselves.

"It must be carelessness on the part of Allah," I thought to myself. "Why did he put so many nasty little insects on this beautiful planet?"

I protected my head with my hands around and walked away from my spaceship for some distance, gradually becoming aware that there was something else unusual: why weren't there any birds in the clear sky? I longed to see a swallow, or even just a little sparrow, which could have eaten all the poisonous mosquitoes that kept attacking me.

可是，在继续探索这个新世界的好奇心的激发下，我却没有用心思考到底是什么原因，不知不觉地离开飞船越走越远，步入了一个阴沉沉的大森林。在这里，我发现了第一个野兽活动的痕迹。

这是一串巨兽的脚印。从它的大小、步距和深陷程度估算，比地球上的大象和犀牛都壮实多了。如果此时此刻我和它在森林小径迎面相逢，必将会带来许多意想不到的麻烦。值得庆幸的是，这串泥地上的脚印已经半硬结了，其间还簇生了一丛丛青草，显然是很早以前留下的“化石”脚印，谁知这种巨兽是否还存在于世间呢？

仿佛是对我作出回答，忽然，我听见林间传来一阵“簌簌”声，一头半鹿半羊状的野兽从我的面前飞也似地蹿跳过去，接着，从对面的树丛里响起“砰”的一声，这头野兽就应声栽倒在血泊中一动也不动了。

这一切很像一场标准的科学幻想电影。我还没有弄清楚是怎么一回事，就从枪声响的地方走出两个装饰古怪的人形动物。和我们不同的是，他们的面孔像刷了一层石灰样的苍

But, urged on by curiosity and eagerness to explore this new world, I did not stop to think of a possible reason for these peculiarities. I wandered further and further away from my spaceship, until eventually I came to a huge and gloomy forest. Here I came across the first signs of animal life.

Those were some footmarks of a huge animal. Judging by their size, the distance between them and their depth, this was an animal bigger and heavier than our elephant or rhinoceros. If I were to meet it face to face on that forest narrow track, I would certainly have been in a great deal of unforeseen trouble. Fortunately, they were evidently made some time ago, since the prints were half obliterated, with tufts of grass growing in them. I wondered whether there were any of this sort of huge creatures still around.

Almost at once, as if in answer to my question, there was a rustling in the forest undergrowth. Then an animal like a cross between a deer and a goat dashed out and sped by me. Immediately afterwards, a gun sounded from the trees beyond me, and the animal fell to the ground and lay motionless in a spreading pool of blood.

It was all very sudden and melodramatic like a SF movie. Before I could make out what was going on, two oddly attired creatures, human in shape, emerged from the part of the forest where the gun had been fired. Of course, they were not actually humans – I could see several differences. Their faces were as pale as though they had been painted with a layer of lime, like the case that they suffered from malnutrition. They had

白，似乎都患了极其严重的营养不良症，后面还拖了一根可笑的长尾巴。尾巴上有布片遮掩，就像穿了一条三脚裤管的长裤。不消说，这是两个到林子里来解闷的猎人。

“喂！”我为终于遇见了这个星球上的智能生物而非常高兴，从藏身的树后走出来，向他们挥手打招呼，可是，我万万没料到这种寻求友谊的表示不仅没有得到应有的报答，相反却招惹了一场天大的祸事。

那两个苍白面孔的猎人瞧见我也吃了一惊。我还来不及招呼第二声，其中一个人就用尾巴稳稳当当地支撑住身子，瞄准我放了一枪，立刻把我打翻在地。他们走到我的跟前，似乎觉得我非常稀奇，叽里咕噜地议论了一阵子，然后取出一根绳子，把我和那头“鹿羊”捆在一起，倒吊在木棍上抬走了。

“这些该死的蛮子！难道是用这种方式来欢迎远方客人的？”我非常气愤，用尽了人间的一切最难听的脏话来咒骂他们。可是这又有什么用处呢？他们根本就不理会我的抗议，反而怪腔怪调地哼起小调来，我无计可施，只好

ridiculous long tails, which were covered with cloth – as though their trousers had three legs. I assumed they were hunters out for a little sport in the forest.

"Hallo!" As I was very glad to discover intelligent creatures on this planet, I stepped out from behind the trees where I had hidden myself and greeted them, waving my hand. It didn't occur to me that this friendly gesture would get me into serious trouble.

The two pale-faced hunters looked surprised when they saw me, but before I could say anything else, one of them, propped up on his tail to steady himself, aimed at me and fired. I was hit, and fell to the ground. They came up and stood before me, apparently amazed at my appearance. They talked for a while in a completely unfamiliar language, and then took out a rope and tied both me and the deer-goat up. They roped us to a wooden pole and then carried us away slung under the pole, with our heads hanging down.

"You wretched savages! Is this any way to welcome a guest from afar?" I was very angry, and I used the strongest language I knew to curse them, but it wasn't of any use. They took no notice of my protests, and just hummed a strange tune as they went. I was at my wits' end, but could do nothing except

耷拉着脑袋，任凭命运女神对我随意摆布。

这段路很远，使我能有机会仔细打量周围的情况。他们也有耕地，但是和森林一样，也很不成样子，使我感到非常诧异的是，除了那头“鹿羊”外，我没有见着别的任何飞禽走兽。可是在田地里，却有成群结队的灰毛老鼠，比希贾拉沙漠骆驼脚夫身上的虱子还多。对于密密麻麻的小虫子肆无忌惮地争食作物叶片时发出的声音，远在几百步外我也能听得一清二楚。在地球上要是遇见这种情况，人们早就逃荒了。从这一阵阵“吱吱喳喳”的昆虫嚼食声中，我开始意识到长尾人的面色苍白的一部分原因。但是我仍然有些不太相信自己的眼睛，怀疑这会不会是一场梦，或者由于我正被倒吊着，天地间的一切观念都颠倒过来？噢，这真是一个迷幻的世界。

我还发现在路上没有机动车，也没有任何畜力车，所有的来往车辆都靠人力拖拉。因此我敢断言，尽管他们已经发明了火药枪，文明程度却远远落后于地球。此外，也进一步判明这个星球上的确非常缺乏飞禽走兽，很可能连

hang my head at the mercy of Goddess of Fate.

They carried me a long way, so I had time to have a good look at the country we passed through. They also had cultivated fields, but, like the forest, the land was in a very poor state. One thing that surprised me was that, apart from the deer-goat, I saw no birds or animals at all, except that in the fields there were hordes of rats – more numerous than the lice in the clothes of camel porters in the Sahara Desert. The buzzing of countless insects as they swarmed over the crops could clearly be heard even from several hundred paces away. If this had been somewhere on earth, it would all have presaged a terrible famine on the way. The sound of the insects eating the crops made me wonder if this was why these long-tailed creatures had such pale faces. But I hardly trusted my own eyes; it might all be a nightmare – or perhaps my ideas were all topsy-turvy as a result of being hung with my head downwards. I felt thoroughly dazed.

I did notice that there were no motor driven vehicles, nor any animal-drawn carts. All the vehicles coming and going were pulled by the long-tailed creatures. So I felt certain that, in spite of the fact that they had invented gunpowder, their civilization lagged far behind that of the earth. It also seemed to confirm that this planet had very little bird and animal life, or they would not have had to pull vehicles themselves, nor would they have had to carry me and the deer-goat with such strenuous effort over such a long distance. I thought it probable

蛇也没有。要不，老鼠和昆虫为什么那样猖獗？怎么会用人拉车，并扛着我和那头“鹿羊”吃力地走老远的路呢？

最后，我被带到一个小镇上，有更多的长尾人拥出来围观，极其兴奋地对我指指点点。在他们的脚下，居然也有许多老鼠到处乱窜。它们从四面八方的墙缝和窟窿眼儿里钻出来，伸长了脖子好奇地窥视我。长尾人似乎对这种可怕的啮齿动物已经习以为常了。有人使劲跺跺脚，或是用富有弹性的尾巴挥赶它们一下。可是不到一会儿，它们又厚颜无耻地围上来了。

长尾人为了看得更仔细，索性把我剥得一丝不挂，放在人丛中拨来拨去地来回观看。当他们俯身检查了我的臀部，发现没有尾巴以后，全部瞪大了眼睛啧啧称奇，活像是真的瞧见了一头罕见的“怪兽”。

我注意到，其中一个留山羊胡子的秃顶老头儿似乎对我特别感兴趣。他边看边记录，还拍了几张照片，不停地用“卡波杜兹”这个词对别人解说，他们听后，就一面点头，一面用尾尖拍地，表示理解和对他的尊敬。

that they had no snakes either, otherwise the rats and insects would not have been so rampant.

At last they brought me to a small town. Here, many more of the long-tailed creatures came to stand round and have a look at me. They kept pointing at me and talking very excitedly. The rats were everywhere, scampering about and getting underfoot. More of them kept appearing, out of cracks and holes in all the walls. They came and stretched out their necks to peer curiously up at me. The long-tailed creatures seemed to be accustomed to these detestable rodents. Some drove them away by stamping their feet or waving their elastic tails, but within seconds the rats would be back again, gathering round me with impunity.

In order to make a thorough examination of me, the long-tailed creatures stripped me naked and stood me among the crowd so that I could be viewed from all directions. When they stopped to examine my buttocks and found I had no tail, they opened their eyes very wide and seemed very much taken aback. They clicked their tongues in amazement, as though they really saw a "strange animal".

I noticed that among them there was a bald old individual with a goatee beard who took a particular interest in me. He was making notes while he inspected me, and then he took several pictures of me. He repeatedly used the term "kaboduzi" to explain something to the rest of the onlookers, who nodded and patted the ground with the tips of their tails – to show their appreciation of what he said and their respect for him.

九死一生

也许正由于很难猎获到一头野生动物，因此那天晚上，面有饥色的长尾人们为此而举行了一场盛大的篝火晚会。他们首先把那头“鹿羊”剥了皮，串在一根铁条上，在火上翻来复去地细细烧烤。

不消说，这时我的伤口非常疼痛，也正饥肠辘辘，一种从未有过的恐怖感笼罩着我，完全没有心思去妄想那诱人的香气和可口的滋味。

“我会不会也落得同样的下场？”我神情紧张地苦苦思考着。我敢打赌，就是我那勇敢的同名祖先在第三次航行时，落在残暴的黑巨人手中时，亲眼瞧见他撕碎了同行的船长塞进嘴巴，也不会比我感到更加恐怖。

我的预感没有错。过了一会儿，果然就有一个老饕客踱了过来，一面馋涎欲滴地咂吧着厚嘴唇，一面用长尾巴轻轻拍打我的肚皮，并提起我的胳膊和大腿来回翻看，像是在品评究竟用什么方法来烹制我似的。最后，他们好像

A NARROW ESCAPE FROM DEATH

I guessed it must have been very rare for the famished-looking long-tailed creatures to capture a wild animal, for that evening they held a grand bonfire party to celebrate their haul. First of all they skinned the deer-goat, spitted it on a metal rod, and roasted it carefully over the fire, turning it again and again.

By this time I was in a bad way. My wound was very painful, and I was extremely hungry too. But I had a horrid fear that I was not destined to enjoy a taste of the delicious-smelling meat.

"Shall I meet with the same fate as that animal?" I wondered, trembling. I felt sure that my brave ancestor, the first Sindbad, never felt as frightened as I did now – not even when he saw his companion the captain torn to pieces and eaten by the cruel black giant on his third voyage.

My premonitions were right. After a while an old gourmand came over to me, smacking his thick lips and drooling with greed. He patted my belly lightly with his long tail, and then lifted my arms and thighs, turning them this way and that as if he was trying to decide which method he would use to cook me. At last they seemed to have made up their minds,

拿定了主意，一个相貌凶恶的家伙提起可怕的厨刀，扭住我的脖子，准备使劲砍下来。我吓得连忙用双手捂住面孔，认为死期已经来临，再也别想瞧见亲爱的巴格达和妈妈了。此时此刻，除非全能的安拉亲自显灵，才能挽救我的性命。

想不到在这个节骨眼儿上，安拉没有出现，那个秃头山羊胡子先生却像天使似地忽然从人丛里钻了出来。

"卡波杜兹！"他挡住了锃光瓦亮的厨刀，手指着我大声呼喊，跟那家伙和一心一意要尝我的肉味的老饕客激烈争论了一阵子，才暂时放过了我。但是从他们那馋得冒出炽烈饥火的目光里可以看出，放弃了这一顿美味的"卡波杜兹"大餐，他们并不是心甘情愿的。我只不过像一条已经被剥去了周身的鳞片的鱼，侥幸从烧得滚沸的油锅里跳出来，总有一天，他们还会把我丢下锅的。

在山羊胡子先生的庇护下，我被带到他的家里，用绳子缚在厨房内的一根桌腿上。

这儿是我的临时牢房，也是老鼠的天堂。山羊胡子先生刚关门走出去，从每一个瓶儿罐儿的后面，都跳出来一

and another fiendish-looking creature raised a terrible kitchen knife; he seized my neck with his other hand, and was evidently about to chop my head off. I was terrified, and covered my face with my hands, thinking that my last hour had come, and that I would never see Baghdad and my mother again. At that point, only a miracle by Allah could save me, I thought.

However, it was not Allah who rescued me on this occasion, but the old fellow with the bald head and goatee, who suddenly appeared out of the crowd like divine intervention.

He checked the downward sweep of the bright knife, shouting at the top of his voice and pointing at me: "kaboduzi!" A heated argument with the gourmands who had intended to eat me ensued, but in the end they spared me for the time being. Judging by their hungry stares they did not willingly give up their delicious "kaboduzi" meal, and I felt just like a scaled fish which has managed to jump out of a pan of boiling oil. Sooner or later, I would be thrown back into the pan again.

I was taken under Goatee's protection to his home, where he tied me to the leg of his kitchen table.

As well as being a temporary prison for me, this kitchen was a paradise for rats. No sooner had Goatee gone out, shutting the door behind him, than great grinning rats jumped

只只龇牙咧嘴的大老鼠，仿佛对我无故侵犯它们的领地很不甘心似的。我深信，这时如果有一只地球上的家猫冒里冒失地闯进来，也准会被这伙凶神恶煞的灰毛老鼠吓破胆，不会比我表现得更加神气些。

过了一会儿，好心的山羊胡子先生又推门走进来。由于不了解我的生活习性，他撒了一把类似玉米粒的谷物喂我吃。在饥饿的驱使下，我皱着眉头勉强吞咽了几粒，实在太干又太硬难以下咽，最后全部被那队劫贼似的大老鼠抢得干干净净，这才使它们的态度变得稍许有些缓和，容忍我蜷缩成一团，在厨桌下占有一小片容身的位置。

面对着鼠群骚动不息的厨房，我在黑暗中想起自己的不幸命运，忍不住哀声吟唱道：

这是梦，还是安拉的魔力，
为什么我被命运抛在这里？
巴格达的阳光，母亲的轻声细语，
都变成了不可回复的记忆。

out from behind bottles and pots, apparently annoyed by my unwarranted intrusion into their territory. I'm sure that even one of our domestic cats, if it had rashly intruded into that room, would have been just as scared by those ferocious grey rats as I was.

Some time passed before Goatee reappeared. He brought me some food, but as he knew nothing of my eating habits he spread something which looked like maize on the floor in front of me. I frowned at this, but driven by hunger I did swallow some with an effort. I soon gave up though: it was too hard and difficult to get down. The result was that the thieving rats ate all of it. After they had finished off the maize they seemed to become more tolerant of me, and allowed me to occupy a small space under the kitchen table by huddling myself up.

As I sat there brooding in the dark, and flinching at the scuffling of the rats, I lamented my miserable fate:

Is it a dream, or the will of Allah?
Why am I abandoned here by Fate?
The Baghdad sun and my mother's soft voice
live on only in my memory.

啊！青春、希望、友谊，
如今都在哪里？
人的尊严受尽了凌辱，
反不如老鼠可以自由来去。
明天，命运将给我带来什么？
是眼泪，是羞耻，还是永远的安息？
唉，不，我想要一双复活的凤凰的羽翼，
飞回遥远的阿拉伯大地。

漫漫的长夜在痛苦和眼泪中过去了。第二天在山羊胡子先生的护送下，我被转送到京城的皇家动物园。在那里，我的出现引起了更大的轰动。每天从早到晚，围着笼子看我的观众挤得水泄不通。“卡波杜兹，卡波杜兹……”他们不停地互相议论着。为了看一眼我这副狼狈相，有的人甚至争先恐后地爬上笼边的几株大树。说真的，当年一只名叫“咪咪”的中国熊猫被送到巴格达动物园的情况，也比不上眼下的这种热闹情况。

Oh, youth, hope, and friendship,
Where are you now?
Human pride is always brought low,
I would rather be one of these rats and have my freedom.
What will fate bring me tomorrow?
Will it be sorrow, shame, or eternal rest?
Oh I want the wings of a phoenix,
To carry me back to far away Arabia.

I passed the whole of that long night in great agony of mind, often in tears. The next day, escorted by Goatee, I was transferred to the imperial Zoo in the capital city, where I created a tremendous sensation. Every day, from morning till night, crowds of the long-tailed creatures packed round my cage. "kaboduzi, kaboduzi," they kept saying, as they talked about me. In order to get a better look at my sorry figure, some of them even fought each other to climb up the trees near my cage. There was greater excitement than when Mimi the Chinese panda first came to Baghdad Zoo.

说起来实在丢脸，堂堂的宇航员居然被关进动物园任人参观。倘若这件事被远在天外的巴格达的朋友们知道了，必定会讪笑得我找一条缝儿钻到地里去。可是我深深理解，这却是那位善心而糊涂透顶的山羊胡子先生目前所能为我争取到的最好待遇了。不管怎么说，总算暂时免掉了厨师的一刀，可以稍稍松一口气啦。

I was deeply ashamed. I – a dignified astronaut – captured and shut up in a zoo as a spectacle! If my friends in far away Baghdad ever found out about it, they would laugh at me so much that I would want to crawl into a hole. But I deeply realized that my present treatment was the best that kind-hearted Goatee could obtain for me. At any rate, I had escaped death under the cook's knife for the time being, which was some comfort.

绝地求生法

我决心利用这个机会进一步探明周围的情况。记得我在巴格达求学的时候，曾被誉为具有语言天才的人，能够用最短的时间学会一门生疏的外语，从深奥典雅的拉丁文到佶屈聱牙的非洲班图语和美洲印第安人的一些语言我无不知晓。如今在这个生死攸关的时刻，我急于了解这些没有礼貌的长尾人对我的处置意见，便竖起耳朵特别注意倾听他们的谈话。

我注意到，他们把那个秃顶老头儿称作"卡波蒂沙儿"，推知"卡波"和"蒂沙儿"分别是"秃"和"老头"的意思。有人手指着隔壁笼子内的一只猴形动物和我对比，曾一再提起"杜兹"这个词。所以我一下子就明白了，这伙长尾巴的家伙把我称作"卡波杜兹"，准是把我当成一只珍奇的"秃毛猴子"了。用同样的方法，我也逐渐掌握了别的一些词汇，弄清了他们的发音和语法的基本特点，能够勉强听懂他们的谈话。从某种意义来说，这个铁笼子反倒

SUPER LANGUAGE SKILL

I decided to try to employ my enforced idleness usefully. At school in Baghdad I was well known for my amazing linguistic talents: I could master a foreign language in a very short time, and I had a good command of the abstruse Latin and knew the awkward Bantu of Africa and the languages of the American Indians. At this juncture of life and death, it would be very useful to me now to learn the impolite long-tailed creatures' language, so that I could find out how they were going to deal with me, so I listened attentively to their conversations.

I found that they called bald old man "kabotishar", and I worked out that "kabo" and "tishar" separately meant "bald" and "old fellow". One pointed at me and compared me with a monkey-like animal in another cage, and repeatedly used the term "duzi", so I understood that by saying "kaboduzi" the long-tailed creature must take me for a precious "hairless monkey". Using the same method I gradually learnt some other words and began to get some grasp of the basic characteristics of their pronunciation and grammar, so that I could barely understand their conversations at last. In a way, my cage served me as a classroom to learn their language,

成了我学习长尾人语言的课堂。但是，这却是一个多么使人心酸和荒唐可笑的课堂啊！

“舒比卡波杜兹，哈拉古里齐，萨尔部斯希里玛拉诺？”一个年轻的长尾姑娘对她的男朋友说。我听懂了，这话的意思是：“这只秃毛猴子真古怪，为什么没有尾巴？”

那个小伙子回答说：“依尔卡修乌斯利其达，比利弗拉维茨古瓦鲁西斯，贝拉乌斯辛卡里尼顿。”意为：“你没有见识过的动物可多啦！去翻一下弗拉维茨的记录吧，被消灭的动物种类数也数不清。”

长尾姑娘又问：“噢，多古弗拉鲁米卡哈诺？”意思是：“啊，抓住它的弗拉得了卡哈吗？”她的男友表示肯定地点了点头。

什么是“弗拉维茨”“弗拉”和“卡哈”？我费了很大的劲儿，才从别的对话中弄清了它们的含义，它们分别是“猎人协会”“猎人”和“奖章”的意思。原来，这个星球上曾经有过许多野生动物，长尾人以狩猎作为最大的生活乐趣。得到法律保护的猎人协会宣布：狩猎可以培养尚武

though it was a ridiculous classroom that I would happily have done without.

"Shubikaboduzi, halagurichi, sarbushisilimarano?" a young long-tailed female said to her boyfriend. I could understand this by now. She was saying, "This hairless monkey is very strange. Why doesn't it have a tail?"

"Yirka- siuwus- lichida, bilifula- wicigu- walusis, beila-wusisinkaliniden," he answered, which meant, "There are lots of animals which you've never seen. If you look in the records of the fulawici you'll see that countless animals have become extinct."

The long-tailed female then said: "Oh, dogufula-lumikahano?" meaning, "Oh, you mean the fula who caught it won a kaha?" and her companion nodded in agreement.

What were "fulawici", "fula", and "kaha"? After much puzzling I succeeded in making out their meaning from other conversations. "fulawici" meant "Hunters' Association", "fula" meant "hunter", and "kaha" meant "medal". I came to know that originally this planet had plenty of wild animals, and the long-tailed creatures regarded hunting as the greatest pleasure in life. The Hunters' Association, which enjoyed legal protection, had declared that hunting fostered martial qualities and was a noble recreation which developed character,

精神，也是一种陶冶性情的高尚娱乐活动！任何人也不得妨碍猎人的活动。每年有定期的全国射猎比赛，优胜者可以获得金光闪闪的大奖章，成为人们羡慕、尊敬，甚至盲目崇拜的对象。自从发明了火药枪以后，在嗜杀成性的猎人们的手中，更增添了一根法力无边的“魔棒”，转眼间几乎就把飞禽走兽杀得一干二净，只剩下为数不多的几只种子动物，陈列在全国唯一的皇家动物园里。我之所以能侥幸保住性命，就是山羊胡子先生根据法律的第二百三十五条第二款：“各种‘种子’动物可保存在皇家动物园里，然其所生育的幼禽幼畜仍须交猎人协会处置。”的规定，要不早就没命了。

由于野生动物日渐稀少，猎获很不容易，所以现在每得到一只，都将在这伙嗜猎成狂的长尾人中成为一次不折不扣的狂欢节，猎人的荣誉显得更高。食谱上经常缺乏脂肪和动物蛋白的长尾人们，莫不以能够分享到一块油汁滴滴的新鲜兽肉为最大的满足。这股疯狂劲儿，我已经在那一次篝火晚会上领教过了。不消说，老鼠、蚊子和别的害虫泛滥成灾，也是野生动物绝灭，使它们失去了各种天敌

so no one was allowed to hinder the hunters' activities. There was an annual national hunting competition, and the winner got a large glistening medal and was admired, respected, and even blindly worshipped by the others. Once firearms were invented, the bloodthirsty hunters, equipped with this mighty "magic wand", killed almost all the birds and animals in a very short period of time, until there were only a limited number of protected species left, which were exhibited in the Imperial Zoo (their only zoo). To save me from death, Goatee had evoked the third provision of Article 235 of their law, which ran: "All protected species must be preserved in the Imperial Zoo but their offspring shall be handed over to the Hunters' Association." Otherwise I lost my life long ago.

As wild animals became scarcer and scarcer, hunting became more difficult, with the result that when an animal was caught it was an occasion for great celebration by the long-tailed creatures, who were still obsessed with hunting, and the hunters were even further honoured. Normally their diet contained practically no meat or animal fat, so it was a tremendous treat for them to get a piece of fresh juicy meat. I had seen their mad thirst for meat on the evening of the bonfire. It was evident that one result of this extermination of wild animals was that rats, mosquitoes, and other pests were completely out of control, since they no longer had any

的结果。

当我刚被关进铁笼子时，曾迫不及待地尽力向前来参观的长尾人们表白，我并不是什么可笑的“卡波杜滋”，而是从天上飞来的外星客人，在我们的家乡有比他们高级得多的文明社会，我的来访将为两个星球之间搭架一座划时代的友谊桥梁。我不能容忍目前的恶劣待遇和种种不堪提及的人身侮辱，他们应该铺上红地毯，鸣放四十八响礼炮，恭恭敬敬地把我接到国宾馆才是正理。要不，这件事若是被我们地球上的同胞知道了，总有一天他们会为此而吃尽苦头的。

“你们这样无礼地对待一个地球人，会感到后悔的！”我气愤地挥舞着拳头，对着长尾人们大声呼喊。

可是，这伙只知道晃荡尾巴的蠢驴根本就不懂，也不愿意去理解我的纯正的巴格达腔的阿拉伯话。我的全部自我表白，连同从我身上剥下来的衣服，都被当作猴类动物的强烈模仿性的充分表现，从而更加认为我是一只猴性十足的古怪动物，引起了长尾人们一场又一场捧腹大笑，并

natural enemies.

When I was first locked up in the cage, I had tried hard to explain to the crowds who came to see me that I was not a ridiculous "kaboduzi" but a guest from another planet in outer space, that my native earth had a much more developed civilization than theirs, and that my visit here was to build an epoch-making bridge of friendship between the two planets. I was deeply resentful of the way they were treating me and of the unbearable insults I endured. They should have been spreading red carpets and firing a 48-gun salute, and respectfully giving me their state guesthouse to stay in. I told them that if their treatment of me ever became known to my compatriots on earth, they would suffer for it sooner or later.

"You'll be sorry for treating an earth man so rudely!" I would shout at them, shaking my fists.

But these tail-waving fools didn't know – and did not even seem to want to know – my standard Baghdad Arabic. Everything I said, together with the clothes they had taken off me, were considered simply a full manifestation of a monkey's great talent for imitation, and they believed even more firmly that I was a strange member of the monkey species. They were always convulsed with laughter at the sight

且因此而挨了几个顽童投掷的石子，额头上肿起了一个大包。

有讽刺意味的是，隔壁笼内的一只母猴反倒对我关心起来了。它隔着铁栅栏轻轻抚摸我的头发，伸出舌头舔吮我的伤口，并且怪腔怪调地学着我的话，龇牙咧嘴地对那些乐不可支的长尾人们尖声咆哮：“你们会后悔的！”不消说，这更加逗弄得那伙自以为是的长尾人如醉如痴，坚信我真的也是一只猴子无疑，招引来更多的观众，使我陷入了更加狼狈不堪的窘境。

我无可奈何地长叹了一口气，坐在笼内回想起踏上这个星球后的种种不幸的遭遇，忍不住双泪长流放声痛哭起来。我这才明白，当初朋友们劝阻我的话一点也不假，安拉的使者的确从来也没有光顾过这个星球。难道我真的命中注定要成为一只“卡波杜滋”，在这儿可耻地了却一生？

除了那只多情的母猴外，所幸山羊胡子先生对我还算和善。他几乎每天都来看望我，总忘不了带一些水果和别的

of my gestures, and their urchins threw stones at me – once giving me a nasty bump on my forehead.

Ironically, it was only the female monkey in the cage next to mine which showed any concern for me. She stretched her hand through the bars to touch my hair, and cleaned my wound by licking it. She imitated what I said, and to the great entertainment of the long-tailed creatures, screeched at them "You'll be sorry for it!" This fascinated the long-tailed creatures who considered themselves always in the right, and naturally confirmed their already firmly held opinion that I was some sort of monkey. More and more of them came to see me, and I was in a state of constant embarrassment.

When I thought of it all I could do was to heave a long sigh. As I sat in the cage I went over all the miseries I had suffered since I came to this planet and I couldn't help weeping bitterly. At last I realized how sensible my friends were to try to dissuade me from my journey. They were right: it was the planet of heathens where undoubtedly Allah's envoy had never set foot. Was I destined to spend the rest of my life here in disgraceful captivity as a "kaboduzi"?

As well as the affectionate female monkey, luckily Goatee was also kind to me. He came to see me almost every day, and always threw me some fruit or other food which he brought

食物丢进我的笼内。在我学会了长尾人语以后，有一天傍晚，游客都已散尽的时候，他愁容满面地来到我的笼前，仔细给我画了一张像，自言自语地喃喃叹息说：“唉，卡波杜兹，这是你的最后一张画像了。”

“为什么？”我感到奇怪地用长尾人的话问他。

“啊，你会说话吗？”他惊奇地瞪大眼睛。可以看出，他是这伙长尾人中最有理智的人，因为他并没有把我的话当成是对猴子的模仿。

由于这个态度，鼓励了我进一步向他表白：“为什么不可以？我是人啊！”

“你真的是一个……人？”他似乎有些不相信自己的耳朵了。

“是的。”我忙不迭地点了点头。

他朝我从头到脚又瞅了一遍，好像还半信半疑，吞吞吐吐地问：“那么……你为什么没有尾巴呢？我仔细检查过你的臀部，证实那儿并没有切除过，你天生就没有高贵的尾巴。”

with him. Then after I had had a pretty good command of their language, one day in the evening when all the tourists had gone, he came up to my cage with a worried look and made a detailed drawing of me. He sighed, and murmured to himself: "Well, kaboduzi, this is my last drawing of you."

"Why?" so I felt curious and asked, in his own tongue.

"What! You can speak?" he exclaimed, his eyes wide with astonishment. It shows that he was the most reasonable individual among all those heathens that he didn't treat my speech as merely a monkey's imitation.

His attitude encouraged me to try further explanation: "Why not? I'm a rational being!"

"You are really a…rational being?" He seemed unable to believe his own ears.

"Yes!" I nodded vigorously.

He scrutinized me from head to foot, and then – still only half believing – asked stammeringly: "Then…why don't you have a tail? I have examined your buttocks most carefully and there is no trace of excision. You were born without the noble tail."

“嗨，你这个糊涂的卡波蒂沙儿。”我感到又好气又好笑地用“蒂沙儿”——老头这个不恭敬的称呼来咒骂他，“人的特征是脑袋，不是尾巴！你知道吗？我来自巴格达，是比你们都聪明得多的地球人。”

为了把意思表达得更清楚，我手指着暮色苍茫的天空对他解说。远处，有一颗星星一闪一闪的，仿佛在用微弱的亮光证实我所说的话。

想不到这时那只邻笼的母猴也来胡搅蛮缠了。它也学着我的样子，手指着头顶的一颗星星，为我帮腔说：“卡坡提沙儿……贝格达……，葱敏的地球人。”这一来，使山羊胡子先生更加茫然了，挠了挠脑袋，瞅瞅我，又瞅瞅那只母猴，弄不明白到底是怎样一回事。

我急了，手指着母猴对他说：“它是杜兹，我是人，你明白吗？”

经过好一阵子的反复解释，最后我陡然想起了，我们的地球科学家曾经说过：“数学是唯一的宇宙语言。”尽管语言和体形都不同，但是有智能的生物，谁能对圆和三

"Oh, you muddle-headed kabotishar!" I felt annoyed and amused at the same time, and used the disrespectful term "tishar" – meaning "old fellow". "Don't you realize that the distinguishing feature of an intelligent creature is its brain, not its tail? I came from Baghdad, one of the earth people, who are much more highly developed than your people."

In order to express myself more clearly, I pointed at the sky through the deepening dusk as I explained. From afar, a star was twinkling as if it confirmed my words with its weak light.

Unfortunately, the female monkey gave me a good deal of trouble at this point. She imitated my gesture, pointing upward, and echoed my words, making sounds like "kabotishar...Paghdad...highly developed earth people..." which thoroughly confused Goatee. He scratched his head, stared at me and then at the monkey, and didn't know what to make of it all.

I became irritated, and pointing at the monkey I said: "That is a duzi; I am a human being. Understand?"

I tried to explain in several different ways before I suddenly remembered that scientists on earth held that mathematics is the only universal language, and that even where speech and bodily forms are different, intelligent beings all have some knowledge of geometric figures – circles, triangles,

角形这些基本的几何图形没有一丁点儿研究呢？为了要证明我和那只母猴并非同类，现在只有借助于泰勒斯、毕达哥拉斯和欧几里得的发明了。我连忙蹲下来，用手指在地上画了一个等腰三角形，画出其恰好平分顶角和底边的中线；又画了一个有内接圆的正方形和五角星形。山羊胡子先生眯着眼睛瞧了一下地上的星形几何图案，又抬头望了一眼天上的星星，他一下子明白了，带着万分抱歉和敬畏的神色向我探问："您真的不是卡波杜滋，是从天上来的一位天使？"

我没有答话，十分矜持地点了点头。

"啊，那太好了！您是天神派来给我们解决危难的。"他隔着笼子紧紧握住我的手。

etc. – so in order to show that I was not of the same species as the monkey I now sought the aid of Thales, Pythagoras and Euclid. I hurriedly squatted down and drew an isosceles triangle on the ground with my finger, showing its vertex angle and the central line on its base side. I also drew a square with an inscribed circle and a five-pointed star figure. Goatee narrowed his eyes as he examined these figures in the sand, and then raised his head and stared at the star in the sky. At last he understood! He asked apologetically, and with an expression of reverence: “You are really not a kaboduzi then but an angel from Heaven?”

I said nothing, but simply nodded in a dignified manner.

“Oh, but that’s wonderful! You are sent by the Great God in Heaven to help in our crisis.” And he grasped my hand tightly through the bars of the cage.

千载良机

原来，皇家动物园的保护者 —— 老国王今天早上驾崩了。明天，王太子就要登基。这位血气方刚的太子热衷狩猎活动，获得过一连串金光灿亮的神射手奖章，是猎人协会的积极赞助者。由于已经没有野生动物可以射猎，他下令在登基日把皇家动物园里的饲养动物全部放出来，举办最后一次盛大的围猎。

王太子宣布说："与其做一个婆婆妈妈的国王，让这些动物关在笼子里无声无息地老死，不如抛掉虚伪的怜悯心，痛痛快快地把它们全部杀光，在历史上留下一个空前绝后的名声。"

为此，他召集了100名全国最有本事的猎人来陪他射猎，还叫来几个白胡子拖地的历史学家，命令他们振作起精神，手握鹅毛笔，准备把王太子和别的猎人每射死一只动物的准确时间和详细情况都记录下来，以便作为历史档案材料永远保存。

GOLDEN OPPORTUNITY

Goatee told me about the calamity now facing his planet. It appeared that the old king – the guardian of the Imperial Zoo – had died that morning and tomorrow the prince would be enthroned. The prince was young and vigorous and very fond of hunting and had won rows of glittering medals as a crack shot. He was an active supporter of the Hunters' Association. As there were no more wild animals to hunt, he had ordered that on his Coronation Day all the animals in the Imperial Zoo were to be let out so that a last grand encircle hunt could take place.

He declared: "I will have nothing to do with theories about compassion for animals. It will be more glorious for me to kill all the remaining animals and thus win unprecedented fame in history, rather than be known as the mawkish king who kept them shut up in cages to die an obscure death from old age."

He had summoned 100 of the best hunters in the country to accompany him on the hunt and had also summoned several oldest and most respected historians with their white beards trailing on the floor, and ordered them to pull themselves together and to write down with feather pens the accurate time and details of each animal shot by the prince and other hunters, so that these records could be kept forever as historical files.

“这样一来，所有的动物就完全绝灭了。”山羊胡子先生对我一五一十地说完情况后，非常伤感地说：“原来我还存有一线希望，依靠这些种子动物来恢复失去了的动物世界，现在可不行啦！”

“别急，有办法了！”我想了一想，头脑忽然一亮，安慰他说，“给我弄一条裤子和一把钢凿来，我就能把所有的种子动物都带走。”

“逃走吗？到处都有发狂的猎人，怎么能逃出他们的手心？”山羊胡子先生不放心地问。

“怕什么！我带你们上天去。”我提议说。

“噢，那怎么行，我们没有翅膀啊！”山羊胡子先生吃了一惊，怀疑自己是不是听错了。

“放心吧，”我劝慰他，“只要我走出这个笼子就有办法，你要相信地球人的本领。”

“真的能够逃出去就好了。我知道一个小岛，岸边都是礁石，谁也没法接近。要是逃到那个岛上就好了。”

这个善心的“卡波蒂沙儿”晃荡着长尾巴，半信半疑

"So all the animals will be completely exterminated," said Goatee sadly, when he had finished telling me the whole story. "I originally had a gleam of hope that the lost animal community could be restored by breeding from the protected specimens. But that won't happen now."

I pondered for a while and then had a brainwave. "Don't worry. I've thought of a way to solve the problem." I consoled him. "Give me a pair of trousers and a chisel and I can rescue the protected animals."

"Rescue? But those mad hunters will be everywhere; how can you escape from them?" Goatee asked worriedly.

"Never fear! We'll escape upwards," I answered.

Goatee was astonished at this and doubted whether he had heard me correctly. "Upwards – oh, that's impossible. We don't have wings!"

I tried to reassure him. "Please trust me. If only I can get out of this cage I can do it. You must have faith in the powers of an earth man."

"If only we really could run away! I know an island whose shore is all reef so that no one can get close to it. If only we could reach it..."

The well-meaning kabotishar, trailing his long tail and half-

地走了。过了一会儿，他带来了我所需要的东西。这时，沉默的黑夜天使已经用它的黑丝绒袍子把整个大地笼罩起来，四周静悄悄的没有一个人影，正是逃跑的绝妙时机。我手握住钢凿，不多一会儿，就凿断了两根铁栏杆，神不知鬼不觉地走出了羁身的笼子。

“快，到森林里去，找我的飞船。”我催促山羊胡子先生说。

为了争取时间，我们穿过一片沙漠抄近路赶去。

夜晚的沙漠静悄悄的，我们踩在松沙地上一步一陷地往前走，一会儿就累得气喘吁吁地提不起脚步了。

“你们这儿有骆驼吗？”我问山羊胡子先生。

“骆驼是什么东西？”他感到不解地问。

“这是沙漠的骄子，风沙和尘暴中出类拔萃的动物呀！”我向他解释说。为了使他懂得我的意思，我在沙地上画了一头骆驼的图形。

山羊胡子先生感到好奇地瞅了一阵子，然后在骆驼头上加了一对短角，背脊上加了两个驼峰，点头回答说：“我

believing, went off, reappearing after a while with the things I needed. By then darkness shrouded the entire planet, it was very quiet and there was not a single soul to be seen. It was an ideal moment to escape. With the chisel I soon cut through two of the bars of my cage and was able to creep through the gap without anyone knowing it.

"Quick – let's go to the forest so that we can look for my spaceship," I urged Goatee.

As we were racing against time, we went by the shortest route, which took us through an area of desert.

The desert was lying silent in the dark. The going was very difficult here – we struggled wearily through the loose sand until we could hardly move one foot in front of the other and were so exhausted that we gasped for breath.

"Do you have camels here?" I asked Goatee.

"What's a camel?" he asked, puzzled.

"We call it the ship of the desert. It's an outstanding animal in soft sand like this or in sandstorms," I explained, and to show him what I meant I drew a picture of a camel on the sandy ground.

Goatee looked at it for a while and then he added a pair of short horns on the head and two humps on the back. He nodded

想起了，从前我们这里也有这样的动物，名叫耶普卡，可以不喝一口水，在沙漠里连走三天三夜，也许比你们的骆驼还有本领。”

“能弄一匹耶普卡来骑吗？”我问道。

“唉，”山羊胡子先生长长地叹了一口气，“它和别的动物一样，也都被猎人剥了皮啦！”

“饲养的牲口也用来打猎吗？”

“没有办法啊！”山羊胡子先生摊开双手，做出无可奈何的姿势，“野生的动物都打完了，猎人们的胃口却还没有满足。猎人协会不是有这么一条规定，任何人也不能妨碍猎人的活动吗？耶普卡就是这样和色拉、诺利斯一起，在火药枪下断绝了子孙的。”

经他进一步解释，我才弄明白，“色拉”和“诺利斯”是类似我们地球上的马和猫的饲养动物。山羊胡子先生非常感慨地说：“该死的火药枪，乒乒乓乓地乱放，总有一天会毁灭我们自己的。”

是的，他说得很对。当所有的飞禽走兽都被屠杀干净，

and said, "I remember now there was such an animal in the past. It was called a yepuka. It could travel three days and nights in the desert without drinking a mouthful of water, which perhaps made it even more useful than your kind on earth."

"Can you get a yepuka for us to ride on?" I asked.

Goatee gave a long sigh and shook his head. "I'm afraid that they have been skinned by the hunters, like all the other animals!"

"Were the domesticated animals also hunted?"

"Yes." He spread out his hands and nodded sadly. "When all the wild animals were extinct, the hunters were still not satisfied, and of course the Hunters' Association stipulates that no one is allowed to hinder hunting activities, so the yepuka together with the shara and the noris were also extinct under their firearms."

By questioning him further I found that the shara and the noris were animals similar to our horse and cat. Goatee said with emotion, "Those dammed guns! The hunters don't care what they do. They'll destroy ourselves one day."

It seemed to me that he was right in this. When all the birds and animals were slaughtered and the natural ecological

自然生态环境的平衡受到破坏以后，谁知道除了老鼠、蝗虫和疟蚊盛行外，还会产生什么灾难性的恶果呢？也许某种看不见的细菌也会趁机发展，最终吞噬掉长尾人本身。

我们默默地并肩走了一段路，我又把话题转到眼下的实际问题："没有了耶普卡，怎么过沙漠呢？"

"是呀，"山羊胡子先生沉思似地回答说，"从那以后，就再也没有人进沙漠了。所以，我们走这条路最近也最安全。"

听了他的话，我沉默了，更加理解他急于要搭救皇家动物园里的最后几只种子动物的心情，这不仅是出于常见的仁慈和同情心，还孕育着一个富有远见的理想。如果不能抢救并繁殖这些残余的种子动物，恢复自然生态环境的平衡，就将给长尾人带来毁灭性的命运。我决心要帮助这个可爱的"卡波蒂沙儿"，咬着牙、使尽最后的气力，和他一起跌跌撞撞地走出了沙漠，终于在密林中找到了我的飞船。谢天谢地的是，这儿十分荒僻，没有人闯进来，飞船还好好地停放在林中空地上。

balance of the species and their relation to the environment was destroyed, who could tell what disastrous consequences would follow, in addition to the plagues of rats, locusts and mosquitoes from which they already suffered? Perhaps some lethal bacteria would be free to develop and would wipe out the long-tailed creatures themselves.

We walked side by side for a while in silence. Then I brought our conversation back to the present practical problem: "How do your people travel in the desert without the yepuka?"

"Well," Goatee answered quietly, "Since then, no one has come into the desert. So this is not only the shortest way but also the safest, too."

I fell silent again, and mused over all he had said as we travelled on. I felt that now I understood better his eagerness to rescue the remaining protected animals in the Imperial Zoo. He was not motivated just by the kindness of his heart but also by a far-sighted ideal. If they failed to rescue and propagate these remaining protected animals, so that the ecological balance could be restored, it could have disastrous consequences for the long-tailed creatures. I felt all the more determined to help this admirable kabotishar. Gritting my teeth, I struggled on. We doddered along, and eventually we came out of the desert and found my spaceship in the thick forest beyond. Thanks to the utter desolation here, no one had intruded and my craft still stood just as I had left it in a patch of open ground in the forest.

瞧见银光闪闪的飞船，山羊胡子先生愣住了。要知道，这个星球的文明整整比地球落后七八个世纪，他虽然是一位博学多闻的“蒂沙儿”，可是也从来没有见识过这样先进的航天器。起初他听我提起飞船，还真的以为是一艘帆、舵、桨、橹都齐全的木船呢！

“这样一艘飞船，怎么能带走全部种子动物？”他感到疑惑地问。

“这好办，”我满不在乎地对他说，“它有足够的马力，就把那些铁笼子都拖上天得啦！”

When he saw the glittering, silvery spaceship, Goatee was stupefied. Remember that the civilization of this planet was seven or eight centuries behind ours on our earth, and erudite "tishar" though he might be, he had never come across anything remotely like an advanced space shuttle. From my referring to it as a 'spaceship' he had expected a wooden ship with sails, helm, oars and a mast.

"How can this flying ship carry all the protected animals?" he asked doubtfully.

"No problem," I said airily. "It is quite powerful enough to lift all the cages into the sky."

临危拯救

我发动了飞船，带着山羊胡子先生，恰好在黎明时分飞回皇家动物园的上空。往下一看，只见园内人头攒动，已挤满了兴高采烈的猎人们，王太子也一身猎装打扮，手持一支镶满了钻石的双筒猎枪，正指手划脚地吩咐手下人，要打开笼子进行最激动人心的一场射猎了。

“快，他们要开笼子了。”山羊胡子先生催促我。

其实不待他嘱咐，我就推动了操纵杆，驾驶着飞船从半空中猛冲下去，巨大的引擎声发出雷霆般的怒吼，那些自以为非常勇武的长尾猎人从来没有见识过现代化的飞船，有的被吓呆了，有的抛掉手中的火药枪四散奔走，王太子本人也一脑袋扎进身后的树丛里，失去了刚才那股耀武扬威的神气。其中居然还有几个胆大的家伙用尾巴撑着地，瞄准我的飞船放了几枪，但这种只能吓唬“鹿羊”和“耶普卡”之类的动物的霰弹，根本就不能对飞船造成任何伤害。当我把飞船下降得更低，紧贴住他们的头皮飞过

A LAST MINUTE RESCUE

I started the engine of the spaceship and in a flash transported Goatee to the sky over the Imperial Zoo. It was just dawn when we got there. Looking down, I could see hundreds of heads below us: the zoo was crowded with joyous hunters. The prince, in hunter's attire, was holding a double-barrelled shotgun inlaid all over with diamonds and as we watched he started gesturing to his men to open the cages in order to begin the most exciting hunt.

"Quick, they are going to open the cages!" Goatee urged me.

But I had already turned back to the controls and drove the spaceship down in a sudden swift dive out of the sky. The thunderous roar of the engines was too much for the long-tailed hunters, who claimed to be so valiant but who had never seen a modern spaceship. Some of them were overcome with fear and some dropped their shotguns from their hands and fled in all directions. The prince ran into the woods behind the zoo, throwing to the winds the courage which he had been boasting about a few moments before. A few people were bold enough to aim and fire at my spaceship, supporting themselves with their tails, but their case shots, which were all too effective against deer-goats and yepuka and other animals, could not damage the spaceship. When I descended still lower so that the spaceship nearly touched

的时候，就全都吓得夹着尾巴逃跑了。

“哈哈！”见到这种情景，我不由地笑出了声。这些愚蠢透顶的长尾猎人也许做梦也不知道，从天上落下来的并不是上帝的惩罚使者，而是受尽了凌辱的“卡波杜兹”，我这才美美地出了一口怨气。

山羊胡子先生对我这一手佩服得五体投地。飞船降落后，我们赶快跳出来，忙不迭地用铁链把关动物的笼子都一个个串连起来。

“卡波杜兹！”当我走出飞船的时候，目光尖利的王太子忽然远远地认出了我，终于明白是怎么一回事了，领先从藏身的地方冲出来，企图活捉我和这只从半空中飘落下来的“大鸟”。

但是他们已经来不及了。气势汹汹的王太子还没有冲到我们的身边，我已经重新发动了飞船，拖带着一串关着各种各样动物的铁笼子飞上了天。倒霉的王太子抓住了最后一个猴笼，打算拖住我们，却反而被飞船带上了天。他的双脚离地以后吓得尖声怪叫，幸好笼内那只多情的母猴紧紧攥住了他，才没有跌下来，乖乖地做了我们的俘虏。

their heads, all of them were so terrified that they ran away with their tails between their legs.

I couldn't help laughing at the sight. Those foolish long-tailed creatures little knew that their visitor descending from the sky was not a punishing angel from their god but the kaboduzi whom they had so humiliated. I was getting my own back with a vengeance now.

Goatee was extremely impressed by my maneuvers. When the spaceship had landed we jumped out and began hurriedly stringing all the cages together with a chain.

Suddenly there was a shout of "kaboduzi"! When I got out of the spaceship the sharp-eyed prince recognized me from his hiding place and began to realize what was happening. He led a charge in an attempt to catch me alive and the "big bird" which had come out of the sky.

But they were too late. Before the overbearing prince could reach us, I had restarted the spaceship and, lifting a string of all the cages of different kinds of animals with us, we rose into the air. The unlucky prince caught hold of the last cage, which the female monkey was in, intending to pull us down, but he too was carried up into the sky by the spaceship. When his feet were whisked off the ground, he screamed with terror. Luckily for him the affectionate female monkey in the cage got a firm hold of him so that he didn't fall. Thus he became our captive.

新诺亚方舟

我们的飞船像是一个空中动物园，在动物嗥叫和长尾人激动的叫喊声中飞出了京城，直朝山羊胡子先生指引的一座孤岛飞去。在那儿，他打算开辟一个天然的动物乐园，重新繁殖野生动物，拯救这个陷入灾难中的星球。

那个骄傲的王太子呢？只好委屈他在这儿吃一点苦头啦！唉！愚蠢的猎人，终于受到命运女神的无情捉弄，颠倒了一个地位，落在野生动物自由自在生存的乐土上了。我深深相信，当他丢失了足以壮胆和称雄的火药枪以后，在这儿或许会变得更加老实、冷静和聪明一些。至于那只多情的母猴会不会放过他这个真正的“卡波杜兹”，就没法一句话说清啦！

“朋友，留在我们这里吧！”善良的山羊胡子先生无限诚恳地要求我说，“在您的帮助下，这个动物乐园一定会管理得更好些。”

“不，我已经想家了。”我轻轻摇了摇头，非常婉转

THE NEW NOAH'S ARK

Like an aerial zoo our spaceship flew out of the capital to the accompaniment of the cries of the animals and the outraged shouts of the long-tailed creatures. We headed for the isolated island, navigated by Goatee, who intended to turn it into a natural animal sanctuary and propagate the wild animals there so that this calamity-stricken planet could be saved.

As to the haughty prince, he had to put up with his situation and make the best of it! The Goddess of Fate had indeed played a malicious trick on this unfortunate hunter, for his status in the free sanctuary of wild animals was reversed. I was firmly convinced that once he was deprived of his shotgun, which had been the prime source of his 'courage' and authority, he would probably become a more honest, sober-minded and wise individual. As to whether this affectionate female monkey would let him – the genuine kaboduzi – off, I could not tell.

"My friend, please stay here!" urged kind-hearted Goatee. "With your help, this animal sanctuary will be run much better."

"No, I am homesick." I shook my head lightly, very politely

地谢绝他，“其实在我看来，管理他们并不难。你只消打开笼子，让它们自由自在地回到大自然里就得啦！我相信下次我再拜访这儿，必定不再是一个没有飞鸟和走兽的寂寞的星球了。”

“你说得对，”山羊胡子先生补充说，“那时，我们的庄稼和森林会长得更好，进沙漠再也不用走路，许多疾病也会消除了。”

我把山羊胡子先生和他的那一大群宝贝儿运送到荒岛上以后，紧紧握住他的手，对他说：“让我再叫您一声‘卡波蒂沙儿’吧，回到地球上，我再也没有机会使用这种语言了。”

山羊胡子先生的眼眶里噙着热泪，宽宏大量地让我用这个不太恭敬的词儿称呼他。可怜巴巴的王太子感到忏悔似地默默走到我的跟前。甚至那只多情的母猴也蹦跳过来，攥住我的衣服，不愿意和我分手。

我轻轻抚拍着它的肩膀，手指着王太子对它说：“亲爱的‘杜兹’，去照顾可怜的王太子吧！他已经放下了猎

declining. "In my opinion it shouldn't be too difficult to run them well. You only have to open all the cages and let them go freely back to nature. I believe when I come to visit here again, it won't be a solitary planet without birds and animals."

"You're right," replied Goatee. "By then our crops and forests should be growing better. We won't have to go across the desert on foot any more, and we will have eliminated many of our present diseases."

So, having delivered Goatee and all his beloved animals to the remote island, I grasped his hand firmly and said, "Let me call you 'Kabotishar' one last time, for when I go back to the earth I shall have no chance to say it again."

Goatee's eyes were brimming with tears and he generously let me use this disrespectful term to salute him. The prince, whom I now felt sorry for, seemed to repent of his former treatment of me and quietly came up to me to say goodbye. Even the affectionate female monkey was bouncing around me and clutching at my clothes to show she was reluctant to part with me.

I patted her lightly on the shoulder and pointing at the prince I said to her, "Dear duzi, go and look after the unlucky prince! He has laid down his shotgun and is no longer a

枪，再也不是恐怖的‘弗拉’了。”

母猴似乎听懂了我的话，真的放开了我，依偎在王太子的身边。我登上了飞船，向山羊胡子先生，向王太子，也向这只热情聪明的母猴挥了挥手，扬起太阳帆，重新飞上了深邃的太空。这次，我的航向非常明确，那是亲爱的地球、巴格达和妈妈……

terrible 'fula'."

The monkey seemed to understand my words and letting go of my hand she went over and snuggled up by the prince's side. I climbed into my spaceship. I waved my hands to Goatee, the prince and the warm-hearted clever monkey. Then I set the sun-sails and started back into the vastness of space again. This time my course was quite certain: I was heading for my dear earth, Baghdad and my mother...

作者简介

刘兴诗 1931年5月8日出生于武汉，重庆南开中学、北京大学毕业。先后在北京大学、华中师范学院、成都地质学院（成都理工大学）等校任教。曾任成都理工大学学科专业建设高级顾问、教授。担任相关学校、研究所之教授，史前考古学研究员，果树古生态环境学研究员。2012年应聘为海南师范大学荣誉教授。

刘兴诗为中国作家协会会员，中国科普作家协会会员，世界科幻小说协会会员。曾任中国地质作家协会副主席、四川省科普作家协会副秘书长、四川省作家协会儿童文学委员会委员等职。

刘兴诗于1945年发表第一篇作品；1952年，开始科普创作；1960年，开始儿童文学创作；1961年，开始科幻小说创作。《美洲来的哥伦布》被评为中国科幻小说重科学流派代表作。

About the author

Liu Xingshi Born in Wuhan on May 8, 1931. Graduated from Nankai Middle School in Chongqing, and Beijing University. Taught at Beijing University, Central China Teachers College, Chengdu Geological College (Chengdu University of Technology) successively. Served as senior adviser and professor for Chengdu University of Technology in discipline establishment; served as professor, research fellow engaged in research of prehistoric archaeology and of ancient ecological environment of wild fruit forest for relevant universities and research institutes. Appointed as honorary professor with Hainan Teachers University in 2012.

Liu is a member of China Writers Association, a member of Popular Science Writers Association, a member of World SF Writers Association. Had been Deputy Chairman of China Geology Writers Association, Deputy Secretary-general of Sichuan Popular Science Writers Association, a member of Children's Literature Committee of Sichuan Writers Association, etc.

Liu published his first article in 1945. He began to write popular science works in 1952, to write children's literature in 1960 and to engage himself in SF writing in 1961. His work *Colombo from America* was regarded as the representative work of the school of SF laying particular stress on science.

截至2012年6月，刘兴诗共出版218本书，发表其他作品数千篇。包括学术论文在内，一些作品被译为英、法、俄等10多国文字。截至2012年5月，获奖140次。

刘兴诗是著名科学家，被认为是四川盆地及邻侧地区地貌、第四纪地层研究权威性专家。他在洞穴考古及古环境学、野生果林古生态环境学和旅游资源开发等方面的研究，做出了突出的贡献，被评价为通晓自然与人文科学、全面发展型学者，并有博物学家的美誉。

Up to June, 2012, he has published 218 titles of works at home and abroad and several thousand pieces of other writings. Some of his works, including his academic theses, have been translated into more than 10 foreign languages, such as English, French, Russian and so on. Up till May, 2012, his works have won 140 prizes.

Liu is a prominent scientist, regarded as a versatile scholar and so is reputed as a naturalist.

译者简介

温绍贤　生于香港，早年毕业于中山大学西方语言文学系。温绍贤是资深翻译家和中英文编辑，翻译和译审的书籍超过100部；他还是长期从事英汉语言比较和翻译研究的学者，有多部学术专著问世；他同时又是小说作家，擅长撰写政经历史长篇小说，代表作有《红的回忆》五部曲和“绿印人”系列三部短篇小说集。现任郑州大学西亚斯国际学院荣誉教授。

在中国图书对外推广网和中国作家协会共同建立的“翻译名家”和“作家档案”网上，均有介绍温绍贤的条目。

有关温绍贤生平的详情，请参阅网上“维基百科”对他的介绍。

英文文字编辑简介

蒂娜·巴莱（Tina Bailey），资深英文译审。

About the translator

Wen Shaoxian was born in Hong Kong. He graduated from the Department of Western Languages and Literature at Sun Yat-sen University. He is a veteran translator as well as a professor of translation and comparative grammar. He has translated and copy-edited more than 100 books of different disciplines. Now Wen is honorary professor with SIAS international University in Central China.

Wen is also a literary writer, expert in writing political and historical novels. His representative works include *Red Memories* pentalogy and *New Immigrants*, a series of three short story collections.

About the English copy-editor

Tina Bailey, veteran English copy-editor.